Moving

Heinemann
LIBRARY

Karen Bryant-Mole

First published in Great Britain by Heinemann Library, Halley Court, Jordan Hill, Oxford OX2 8EJ
a division of Reed Educational & Professional Publishing Ltd.

OXFORD FLORENCE PRAGUE MADRID ATHENS MELBOURNE AUCKLAND KUALA LUMPUR
SINGAPORE TOKYO IBADAN NAIROBI KAMPALA JOHANNESBURG GABORONE PORTSMOUTH
NH (USA) CHICAGO MEXICO CITY SAO PAULO

Designed by Jean Wheeler
Commissioned photography by Zul Mukhida
Consultant – Hazel Grice
Printed in Hong Kong / China

02 01 00 99
10 9 8 7 6 5 4 3 2 1

ISBN 0 431 07837 8

This title is also available in a hardback
library edition (ISBN 0 431 07832 7).

British Library Cataloguing in Publication Data

Bryant-Mole, Karen
  Moving. - (Science all around me)
  1. Motion - Juvenile literature 2. Kinematics - Juvenile literature
  I. Title
  531.1'1

A number of questions are posed in this book. They are designed
to consolidate children's understanding by encouraging further
exploration of the science in their everyday lives.

**Words that appear in the text in bold can
be found in the glossary.**

Acknowledgements
The Publishers would like to thank the following for permission to reproduce photographs: Bruce Coleman 8 (Gunther Ziesler), 18 (J. Brackenbury),
20 (Jane Burton); Eye Ubiquitous 14 (Steve Lindridge); Positive Images 12, 22; Tony Stone Images 4 (Daryl Balfour), 10 (James Balog); Zefa 6, 16.

Every effort had been made to contact copyright holders of any material reproduced in this book. Any omissions will be
rectified in subsequent printings if notice is given to the Publisher.

Contents

Animals

All animals can move. They need to move to find food to eat and somewhere safe to rest.

They may need to escape from other animals. This elephant had to move to find the water it is drinking.

 *Human beings are animals, too.*

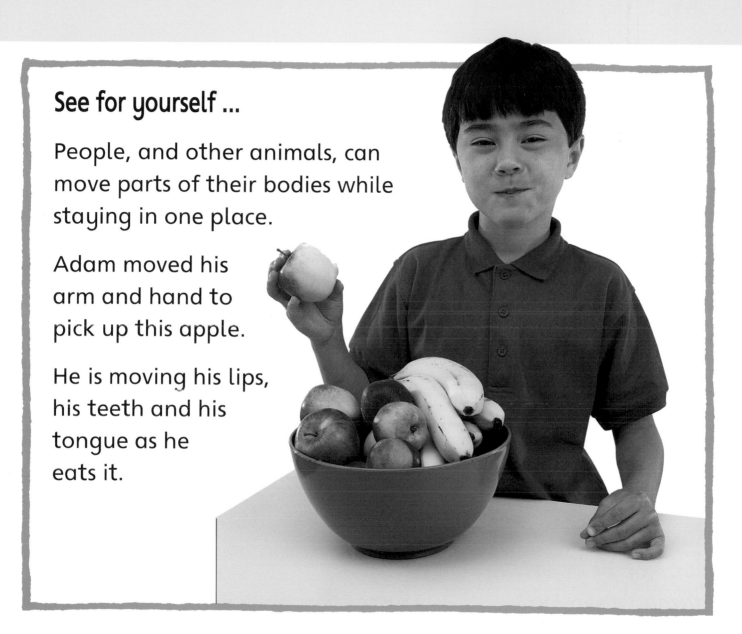

See for yourself ...

People, and other animals, can move parts of their bodies while staying in one place.

Adam moved his arm and hand to pick up this apple.

He is moving his lips, his teeth and his tongue as he eats it.

Skeleton

Lots of animals have a skeleton. A skeleton is a frame that gives the body its shape and allows it to move.

This antelope and her baby have a skeleton that is made up of bones.

? *Can you see some of the mother antelope's bones through her skin?*

See for yourself ...

Bartie is trying to feel his skeleton. His hands are on his ribs.

He has long bones in his arms and legs and lots of little bones in his hands and feet.

His **spine** is made up of small bones that allow his back to bend.

Joints

Animals' bones are linked together at places called joints.

Joints in this ape's arms and legs allow them to bend, so that the ape can climb up the tree.

(i) *Some joints let the bones move backwards and forwards. Other joints let the bones twist and turn, too.*

8

See for yourself ...

Our joints let us bend and twist our bodies. Jessica is trying to bend in as many places as she can!

She is using joints in her ankles, toes, knees and hips.

She is also using joints in her fingers, wrists, elbows, shoulders and neck.

Muscles

Bones do not move by themselves. They are pulled into different positions by **muscles**. The more a muscle is used, the stronger it becomes.

This tiger does a lot of running and jumping. It has **developed** large, strong leg muscles.

 Muscles can only pull. They cannot push.

See for yourself ...

Some of our muscles are large and some are only small.

Melissa can feel the large muscles in her arm pulling as she lifts up this heavy bag.

Lots of tiny muscles in her face are pulling it into a big smile!

Air, land and water

The type of body an animal has depends on how and where it moves.

These ducks use their legs and feet to walk on land and swim through water. They use their wings to fly through the air.

(i) *Ducks have special feet, called webbed feet. These help them to swim.*

See for yourself ...

Emerich is putting some model animals into groups.

One group of animals moves over land. One group can fly through the air. The other group can swim through water.

13

Flying

Almost all birds can fly. They fly by flapping their wings or by gliding.

Flapping helps to push the bird through the air.

Gliding is like floating on the air. Instead of flapping its wings, the bird keeps them stretched out.

Can you think of any birds that can't fly?

See for yourself ...

Birds' wings are a special shape.

They make the air move more quickly over the top of the wings than underneath. This helps to lift the bird into the air.

Berta is testing this by blowing along the top of a strip of paper. As she blows, the paper lifts up.

Swimming

Fish swim by moving their tails from side to side.
This pushes the fish through the water.

Many fish have **fins** on their bodies. These fins allow the fish to **steer** in the direction it wants to go.

(i) *Some animals, like frogs, use their legs to swim.*

See for yourself ...

Jonathan is using a wind-up bath toy to see how a flapping tail can push a fish through water.

He has wound up the bath toy and put it in the water. As the tail flaps from side to side, the bath toy moves forwards.

Legs

This young **locust** uses its legs to jump from place to place. Kangaroos and frogs move by jumping, too.

Other animals use their legs to run or walk.

Some, like tortoises, move slowly. Others, like cheetahs, can move very quickly.

? *How many legs does an **insect** have?*

See for yourself ...

Berta is counting all the ways she can use
her legs to move from one place to another.

So far, she has hopped, run, walked, jumped
and skipped.

Now she is crawling.

Moving without legs

This earthworm moves by squashing up and stretching out different **sections** of its body.

Many snakes wriggle along the ground, by bending to one side and then the other.

(i) *Earthworms have lots of tiny **bristles** under their bodies, which help them to grip the earth.*

See for yourself ...

Snails slide along on a strong muscle.

Melissa has
put a snail
into a small
plastic tank.
She is
watching the
snail as it moves
up the side.

If you try this, remember
to put the snail back where
you found it.

Plants

Plants can move parts of themselves, too.

Some plants close up their petals at night.
This photograph was taken in the evening.
The plants are just starting to close up their petals.

Some plants also close up their petals when it is cold or wet.

See for yourself ...

Green plants need sunlight to make food for themselves.

Adam put this plant on a windowsill for a few days. All the leaves are now facing in the same direction.

They moved themselves into this position so that they could catch as much sunlight as possible.

Glossary

bristles short hairs

developed grown

escape get away from something

fins flaps that stick out

insect a small animal with six legs

locust a type of insect

muscles bundles of thin bands that move parts of the body

sections parts of something

spine backbone

steer go in a particular direction

Index